PERFECT
POTS

Simon Akeroyd

 National Trust

First published in the United Kingdom in 2019 by
National Trust Books
43 Great Ormond Street
London
WC1N 3HZ

An imprint of Pavilion Books Company Ltd

ISBN 978-1-91135-870-1

A CIP catalogue record for this book is available from the British Library.

10 9 8 7 6 5 4 3 2 1

Reproduction by Mission Productions Ltd, Hong Kong
Printed in Italy by Elcograf S.P.A.
This book can be ordered direct from the publisher at www.pavilionbooks.com

Interior illustrations by Abi Read

CONTENTS

INTRODUCTION

In an increasingly urban world not all of us have the luxury of a patch of earth to cultivate next to our houses. It may be necessary or desirable to live in a flat or apartment, or to have only a paved area to call our own outside our back door, yet there is increasing evidence that having some sort of interaction with nature is good for our physical and mental wellbeing. This is especially important with the modern trend towards busy, technologically advanced lives. So it goes without saying that, for many people wanting to garden, growing plants in containers is the only practical option possible.

As a healthy diet is becoming an increasing concern, growing fresh produce is also something that people are turning to more and more in their search for a better life. While for some people, an allotment is the perfect antidote to the stresses of modern existence, for others the time and cost involved may simply not be suitable. But there is no reason why you can't have your own mini-allotment at home, even if it lives on your kitchen windowsill.

Even those with beds and borders galore will probably still have a need for containers of some sort or another. A porch can be made much more welcoming with well-planted pots sitting either side of the entrance, or a hanging basket display to delight visitors. Meanwhile, bigger, dramatic containers can provide the most wonderful focal points in a garden display, at much less cost than a piece of garden furniture or a statue. Whether they sit at the end of a path, or form the centrepiece of a border, they will add a whole extra dimension to your garden.

The single biggest advantage to growing plants in containers is flexibility. A border is, by its very nature, fairly static. No matter how good a designer you are, there will be times when a shrub has finished flowering or a perennial is dying down and you are left with a lean space. Popping a thriving container display into the mix can make a real difference to the overall look, brightening up and helping to disguise any ugliness.

Containers, unless they are really huge, can generally be easily moved. You can shift plants around without having to go through the rigmarole of digging them out and potentially doing them a great deal of harm, or at least having to cut them back hard.

With a container it is possible to add or subtract much more easily. Lilies are a perfect example. Planted in plastic pots and brought into flower in a glasshouse or cold frame, they can simply be plunged into a spare space in a planting scheme, and allowed to flower before being removed to spend their time dormant and dry, hidden out of sight. This is especially useful in areas of high winter rainfall where the bulbs can easily rot.

So too can the planting in containers be changed much more easily. A window box of tulips can be quickly replanted with fresh summer bedding for a completely new look. If you only have a few pots, changing the planting to reflect the seasons will make your display much more worthwhile and interesting. Pots that are not looking so good can be hidden away to complete their dormancy.

Containers also allow you to grow plants that your own garden conditions will simply not support. Many people would like to grow camellias or other acid-loving plants, but do not have the soil conditions to support these tricky beauties. Chalky soil, especially, is anathema to acid-loving plants and will cause interminable decline in their health and vigour. Instead of a thriving plant covered in flowers you will end up with yellowing leaves and stunted and weak growth, if not a slow death. However, a container filled with the right sort of compost, in this case ericaceous compost, will provide that one specific condition that is missing in your garden. The same is true of water. You may really want to grow alpines but if your soil is wet and damp through the winter, only a container with the right mix of well-drained, gritty compost will allow this. And of course the opposite is also true; if water is all you desire, a half-barrel can be sealed and planted up to make a mini-pond where a larger pond in your garden is not possible.

Containers offer a practical solution to other specific problems, too. Plants with a reputation for uncontrolled spreading, such as some forms of bamboo or mint, should be containerised before planting to reduce the incidence of spread. If they are in appropriately sized containers both these plants can be dropped into a hole in the ground and kept in check much more easily than if they were planted directly into soil.

Similarly, growing indoors is only possible with containers of some sort or another, whether this be simple ceramic decorative pots for indoor plants, or the most up-to-date indoor growing technology designed to supply fresh food for your kitchen. Hydroponics, artificial light and irrigation have been used by professionals for years but are now making their way into the general market.

Finally, containers can be a practical solution for people with mobility or disability issues who may have trouble with the physical activity involved in planting and maintaining a bed or border. Raising beds or pots to a suitable height means that many more people can enjoy gardening.

Whatever your reasons for wanting to use containers in your gardening adventures, there are some simple rules and tips to follow that will ensure your displays look good, stay healthy and show the world that you clearly have 'green fingers', figuratively speaking at least.

THE
BASICS

A standard 'lollipop' bay tree looks great in a formal garden.

CONTAINERS THAT REFLECT YOUR STYLE

The same design principles apply to containers as to gardening generally. Whatever your style – formal or informal, stylish or more relaxed – containers can fit in with any scheme, either adding to the overall feel or, if you have the confidence and an eye for surprise, accentuating by difference the overall design.

Formal-style gardens are characterised by order and symmetry, clean shapes and lines, often with repetition. Containers are a brilliant way to further emphasise such a style, especially when it comes to symmetry and repetition, by providing easily recurring elements. Symmetrical pots and matched planting either side of a path or door provide a sense of order and formality. With strong geometric container shapes and architectural planting the effect is even stronger. In the most design-led stylised gardens, pots and containers almost inevitably make a huge contribution to the overall look, including everything from pleached trees to yuccas and bamboo. Clipped box and topiary shapes are a classic choice and almost an essential part of a good formal garden scheme. This is a style that works well near modern buildings, workplaces and in public urban areas.

Informal design is obviously more natural-looking, and generally suits those with less time or a more relaxed lifestyle and outlook. Family gardens tend to be more informal, allowing children, pets and guests to spend time doing the things they love. Containers here can be colourful and cheerful or overflowing with billowing prettiness, softening and disguising all manner of practical but ugly things. They may be useful, containing herbs, vegetables or fruit for the kitchen, educational or wildlife-friendly, or just carefully placed so that even in the depths of winter they can bring some cheer to those relegated to looking out of the window. They are extremely useful too for safeguarding treasured plants, which if planted out in a bed or border could easily be damaged by wandering children and pets.

Informal gardens also suit non-traditional containers, such as old sinks, salvaged items, recycled pallets, buckets and all manner of 'found' objects.

Lavender in an informal container.

SELECTING THE RIGHT CONTAINER

Ultimately, container selection is down to personal choice and taste. Nevertheless, there are a few ground rules to consider when buying or making something that will hold plants.

Size is an essential factor. There should always be enough growing space for a plant to thrive. Containers should be big enough to hold an adequate amount of growing medium, and to allow some freedom to grow. They should also allow the free drainage of excess water. It is surprising how often pots are sold with no drainage holes at the bottom, leading to waterlogging, and certainly this is something that can be an issue with recycled objects. Style and cost are the other major factors involved in container choice.

The classic container material is terracotta. Unglazed terracotta pots have been a staple of the British garden for centuries, hand-thrown in the Victorian and Edwardian era, but now usually machine-made. The colour of terracotta works perfectly with every plant combination and it can be used in

both formal and informal settings. Larger terracotta pots often come with gentle decoration or engraving to add extra interest without taking centre stage and outcompeting the plants themselves. Terracotta pots are porous and do absorb some water (useful if you have a tendency to overwater) as well as minerals, but have a reputation for keeping plant roots cooler in summer and warmer in winter as a result of this porosity. Their big disadvantage is that they can break rather easily, although broken pieces make excellent crocks for the bottoms of other container displays.

If the earthy colours of terracotta are not for you, these pots can easily be painted for a more individual look. Specialist clay paints are available, or try one of the newer multi-use garden paints to tone your pots with your shed, summerhouse or garden furniture, although be aware that the paint tends not to be very long-lasting. Masonry paint is also a possibility for a classic, formal, matching look.

If you have the urge for something more creative and unique, or want a specific design, use acrylic paints to add patterns or artistic scenes before covering with a double layer of matt varnish to protect your work from the elements. Avoid using brighter green shades as these inevitably tend to look brash against the more natural colour of foliage.

Old terracotta pots are increasingly difficult to come by as they are very sought after, especially those that have a handmade look

Terracotta pots can be
'aged' using yoghurt.

about them. As terracotta ages it develops a patina that softens the colour to a sort of dusky pink, as well as a delicious natural decoration of marks, mineral spots, moss and even lichens, denoting the passage of time. While nothing beats the dignity of age, there are some tricks you can pull to artificially age your pots and reduce the harshness of their new appearance. Painting on yoghurt and leaving your pot in a sheltered, moist place for a month or so will give it a natural patina that mimics the results of mineral and organic ageing. The same effect can be achieved even more quickly by soaking a pot in heavily salted water and leaving to dry, but terracotta's natural tendency to absorb minerals, in this case, could be dangerous for your plants, which will not cope with the high salt levels that may leach out into the compost, so this is only recommended if the plant can be protected by another inner pot.

More decorative glazed pots are now available in a range of styles, from traditional Chinese designs, perfect for displaying bamboo, and faux antique styles, to more modern shaped pots in a variety of colours. Design-wise it is easier to keep to one style of pot in a display where you are combining pots together, but you can ring the changes by using similarly decorated pots of different shapes and sizes for a more informal but unified effect. For formal designs, pots in the same size and design are preferable to ensure that order and symmetry are maintained. Unless you are planning to bring your pots in for the winter, check that they are frost-resistant; the more decorated pots will often crack in cold weather and may need extra protection.

The biggest issue with terracotta pots is weight, so, if you think you might want to move large pots from time to time, it is worth investing in wheeled pot movers to avoid unnecessary lifting.

Plastic containers are often much cheaper to buy but rarely last as long as their stone and terracotta counterparts. One obvious advantage is that they tend to be less heavy, so may be a better choice for anyone with a mobility or disability issue. Unlike

A wheeled pot mover is invaluable for relocating larger pots.

terracotta, plastic does not absorb water or minerals and cannot protect roots so well, but its ability to hold water is useful for people of a forgetful nature or those with less time on their hands. In full sunlight, however, plastic can often become brittle and crack, and black pots will absorb more sunlight than others, which may cause a real problem for plants that are not drought- and heat-tolerant, so be careful about your placing.

Plastic, of course, can come in any colour imaginable and in a very wide variety of shapes and sizes. At its most basic, even the humble grow bag is just a plastic, pillow-shaped container, designed to be cheap but functional, but generally speaking most people prefer containers that are a little more aesthetically pleasing. Bright colours look very jolly and fit well into chic or quirky urban designs, while the less interesting ones are easy to disguise with clever planting, allowing tumbling plants to grow over and down the sides to make the containers less conspicuous.

If rooftop or balcony gardening is your thing, using plastic containers will help to minimise the weight, as this can be a real potential issue if you are planning to fill your space with pots.

If you are prepared to pay a little more, plastic containers are now available that mimic much more expensive materials, such as stone and marble. The best are extremely good-looking, and are generally cheaper and lighter than their genuine counterparts.

Real stone, metal and wood containers are probably the most expensive types of container you can buy, but they last for a considerable period of time so can be considered an investment. Otherwise, fibreglass or fibreclay containers are often made to look like something more expensive and are generally of a higher quality than their plastic equivalents, but cheaper than the real thing.

It is quite easy to get hold of wooden barrels or half-barrels left over from alcohol distilling and storage. These are perfect for a rustic feel, already having a lovely patina of age, as well as a distinctive smell, and can come in a range of sizes. The biggest, when filled with compost and plants, will become extremely heavy and moving them may cause damage both to the barrels and your back, so make sure you place them where they can sit undisturbed. Half-barrels are also a popular choice for making a container water feature, although they will need to be made watertight first.

For a formal setting, wooden planters based on the famous 'Versailles' design are very popular. Originally designed by André Le Nôtre, the gardener who created the extraordinary gardens at Versailles, these containers were used to display and move the thousands of citrus trees that adorned Louis XIV's garden in the summertime. Today, although they are less about practicality, they have retained their classic appeal. Versailles planters are characterised by their square shape and the finials (entirely decorative) that adorn each corner.

Square wooden planters for vegetables and fruit are easily made if you have access to wood and tools, or they can now be bought fairly cheaply, as can taller planters for people who may have trouble bending. If it is not already protected do give the wood a coat of preservative to extend its working life.

Stone and metal are the most enduring materials for containers, hence fabulous antiques can still be found, at a price, in architectural salvage yards and from specialist suppliers. Most of us, though, may have to content ourselves with imitations. Lead planters confer a definite gravitas in formal settings, fitting in well with both old and new designs, while copper is bang on trend, working well with the fashion for industrial chic. Metal containers should be lined to prevent any contamination of the potting medium and reduce the effect of heat retention, which could scorch roots. One fashionable option is to use concrete, again as a nod to design trends, but this is inevitably very heavy so best used for permanent arrangements. For a luxurious look real stone, such as marble and sandstone, cannot be beaten.

For those on a budget or who prefer to express their individuality more uniquely in the garden, all manner of objects and items can be used as planters. Just about anything that can hold potting medium has potential, the main criteria being that it drains away excess water, or at least can be converted in some way to do this. From old tyres to bicycles, welly boots to buckets, teacups to toolboxes, old cars to bathtubs, gardens everywhere are full of quirky and unusual items overflowing with plants. This is an idea that is perfectly suited to more informal gardens, as well as being an excellent and fun way to get kids or unwilling partners involved in gardening. Repurposing unwanted items makes perfect sense when resources are so limited and waste is such a huge issue for the environment, with the added bonus that the plants growing in them are contributing to a healthier atmosphere.

To convert an unwanted item into a plant container you may have to create drainage holes before using. It is relatively easy to drill most materials, even ceramics, with the right drill bit. Masking tape applied over the surface you are planning to drill will give you a more secure grip and is a useful trick on shiny surfaces. Items that already have holes, such as sieves or colanders, may need to be lined with black plastic to stop compost falling out, although this too will need to be pierced to allow water to drain.

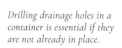

Drilling drainage holes in a container is essential if they are not already in place.

POTTING COMPOST AND ADDITIVES

Most compost that is readily available in garden centres is sold as 'multi-purpose' and is a sort of jack-of-all-trades basic mixture that will do the job. However, when it comes to the highly artificial and constrained environment of the container, it is worth spending a little more time and money supplying a growing medium that is properly matched to your plant's needs. Though specialist container compost is often available and works well for many plants, you may also need to modify your potting medium to ensure that specific groups of plants can thrive.

Ordinary garden soil, while it is free, is rarely worth using. It can be variable in nature, will probably contain weed seeds and diseases and may not have the necessary characteristics needed for successful container growing. If it is used it should be sterilised first, in a microwave or oven, making it difficult and costly to process in larger quantities.

A good container compost should be moisture and oxygen retentive while able to cope with heavy watering. Nutrients are also a big issue. Because containers need a higher level of watering, nutrients will leach out much more quickly and may not be replaced through natural processes. In the ground your plants may be able to access nearby nutrients through the actions of micro-organisms in the soil, as there is increasing evidence that the soil and the plants growing in it are all part of a complex, connected distribution web. This is not so for a plant in a pot. It is up to the gardener to provide the extra nutrients.

Bought compost comes in two basic categories: loam-based or loamless. Loam-based composts have a high proportion of loam, sterilised soil that forms the basis of the mix, along with a variety of other ingredients. They drain well but are slower to dry out completely and have a good open structure that encourages root development. They help to retain nutrients for longer too. As loam-based composts are heavier than their loamless counterparts they are often recommended for plantings that may be quite top-heavy. Container-planted trees, for example, tend to be disproportionately heavier and larger at the top than the bottom so can easily tip over in a light pot (especially if not watered). The extra weight of loam-based compost can help prevent this. They are recommended for longer-term plantings in general as they degrade less quickly, and it is also much easier to transfer a plant from a loam-based compost into the ground in the event that you choose to replace your container displays.

The most common mixes of loam-based commercially available composts are based on the formulas created by the John Innes Institute, named after the wealthy property developer whose money funded its creation. These have been developed scientifically and each recipe has a specific use: John Innes No. 1, with low nutrients, is for seed sowing and cuttings; No. 2 for potting on and standard potting; while No. 3, usually the most useful for container growing, has the highest levels of nutrients and is suitable for plants with greater needs, such as those constricted by containers.

You can also use the formula to make your own compost, as long as you can obtain the correct ingredients. The formula does include peat, but it is possible to find a peat substitute to replace this to prevent damage to the environment.

Loamless composts are based much more heavily on peat or peat substitute. They are clean and light and usually cheaper, but the heavy reliance on peat is a definite drawback if you care about wider environmental issues, so do look for mixes that contain peat substitute rather than the real thing, the harvesting of which is having a devastating effect on our landscape and environment. Peat substitutes include leaf mould, coir (coconut fibre) and fine bark.

Loamless composts are moisture retentive but if allowed to dry out completely are much more difficult to re-wet. Once dry they should really be gently soaked in water, which can be difficult with larger pots. Ideally it is always best to water them consistently. This tendency to dry out also means they shrink and contract, and since they also tend to degrade fairly quickly, they may not be a good long-term option for your plants. For short-term use, though, such as seasonal displays of planters or baskets, loamless composts are perfectly suitable, and their lightness is a definite bonus for anything hanging.

It is also possible to buy more specialist composts for specific plant groups. Ericaceous compost has been designed for acid-loving plants, such as azaleas, rhododendrons and blueberries, while vegetable-growing compost with added specific nutrients is often available during the growing season, mostly but not exclusively in grow bags. Bulb, orchid, hanging basket and water plant compost can also be bought from good garden centres.

Specialist composts have ingredients added to a basic mix to modify their effect, but there is no reason why gardeners cannot modify their own mixes, and there are a number of additives, bought or homemade, that can be useful.

Extra nutrition, especially for loamless compost, can be added in before planting, whether you choose bought inorganic slow-release fertiliser or more environmentally friendly ingredients, such as worm compost, seaweed meal or homemade comfrey leaf mould.

Grit and grit sand keep soil structure open and free-draining, and this is pretty much essential when planting alpines, and also for drought-tolerant plants such as succulents and cacti. Buy horticultural, washed sand to prevent any harmful minerals leaching into the compost, and do not be tempted to use beach sand, which will inevitably be covered with large quantities of salt that will burn plant roots.

Vermiculite and perlite are inert granules of treated rock and mineral that are often added to potting composts to help with water retention and keep an open structure. The main difference between the two is that perlite holds more air and vermiculite more nutrients, but in many cases they can be interchangeable. For plantings where water retention may be a real issue, such as summer bedding displays in hanging baskets, water-retaining gels or granules can be added. These act like tiny reservoirs, expanding and holding on to water for plants to use.

Standard leaf mould is a useful addition for woodland plants.

POTTING – THE BASICS

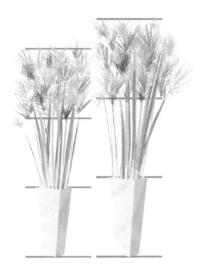

Plants that are twice the height of their container always look good.

Basic design

The principles of design apply just as much to container growing as they do to the wider garden. Try to match containers and planting so that the two complement each other and fit in with the style and look of your garden. Proportion is a key feature. As a rule of thumb, two-thirds planting height to one-third pot height makes for a classic composition that naturally pleases the eye. Generally groups of three and odd numbers seem to hold sway when it comes to aesthetics, in gardening as much as in art, unless you are aiming for symmetry, which requires multiples of two and mirror imaging to be successful.

Colour can also play a vital part in achieving the appropriate look for your garden. A riot of colour works well in the summer months if done with style and abundance, producing a jolly seaside B&B effect, but in most cases, keeping to a good design palette is the best plan. Harmonious tones based on one colour look elegant and refined, while for something more daring try combinations of three different colours. Two main colours with a third accent colour always looks good and is a useful trick to have up your sleeve.

As a general rule, the larger the pot or container the better. Not only is this more practical, as it will reduce the need to water quite so frequently, but your plants will have room to grow for longer, reducing the need to repot, and you will avoid the look of fussiness and clutter that often results from lots of small pots dotted around randomly. However, it is still the case that a small plant in a big pot will not look particularly attractive and may become waterlogged with the excess water that a big pot can hold, so use your common sense. Small, diminutive plants, such as alpines and spreading succulents, need a container that emphasises the miniature sense of scale, while a single architectural specimen plant needs a more striking, taller, bigger pot, which will emphasise the 'wow' factor.

Siting pots and containers also requires some thought and attention. There are both practical and aesthetic considerations to take account of. The right conditions for the plant are key, whether this be cool shade or hot sun, for example. Of course, one of the great advantages of container growing is the relative ease of movement if the conditions do not suit your plants. The famous Versailles planter was invented for the eponymous gardens initially as a solution to moving thousands of expensive citrus trees from their summer position on the terraces to their winter rest under glass, protected from harsh weather.

For plants that are likely to need regular watering, placing them close to a water source will save you considerable time and energy, and make it more likely that you will take care of them. You may also want to consider the value of your container. A fine antique piece or sculpted pot may be a temptation to a thief if positioned where it can be easily taken, so think carefully about placement, or anchor it in some way to avoid a nasty surprise.

Aesthetically containers have many uses in the garden. They are excellent for marking boundaries and for softening hard lines or shapes. A line of containers against an ugly fence will make a useful distraction, as will a plethora of pots attached to a nondescript wall. Containers can mark out specific areas, letting everyone know where the dining area of the garden is, for example, or where children can play or an informal, relaxed area can be found.

In many gardens without the benefit of a fantastic landscape outside the walls or room for a tree or sculpture, a pot or container can make a perfect focal point, emphasising a vista and even making your garden look bigger. Focal points help us to make more sense of a garden, giving our eyes somewhere specific to land rather than trying to take the whole view in at once. Whether this is in the centre of a square patch, at the end of a path or slightly off-centre to make things more interesting, it is worth using a prop of some sort, like a cane or a chair, to check the appropriate position and scale by eye before finally placing your pot into position.

Safety issues

On balconies and roof gardens weight is a big issue. When full of wet compost containers can become surprisingly heavy, so take this into account when designing your scheme in these particular areas. There is also a greater risk of wind damage the higher up your garden is, and this too needs to be taken into account when making your container choices.

Last but not least, place containers where they will not be a trip hazard, especially on roofs and balconies, and make sure that any containers at height are securely fixed.

Use harmonious colours for a restful effect.

Use crocks at the bottom of your pot for drainage.

BASIC PLANTING INSTRUCTIONS

Long-term plantings

Plants that are likely to be kept in a pot on a permanent basis, or at least for the foreseeable future, such as shrubs or trees, are treated a little differently from seasonal planting displays.

Begin by assembling everything you need: the container; broken pot pieces (known as crocks) to ensure good drainage; a good loam-based compost; slow-release fertiliser; any plinth or feet that you plan to use for the pot; and the plant itself. If the container is large place it into position, along with any feet, before starting to plant it up as it may well be too heavy to move afterwards. Whatever kind of plant you are using make sure to give it a good water before you plant it.

Begin by putting in a good layer of crocks, which will both help drain excess water and stop too much soil from washing away. You can also add a layer of gravel if the pot is large enough. Fill the pot to around half its depth with compost, mixed with slow-release fertiliser, then place your plant, still in its container, into position and fill any remaining space up to just below the rim. Firm in gently before removing the plant and taking it out of its pot. Tease out the roots a little, then place the plant back in the hole before firming in gently, ensuring that there are no air holes. Always water well immediately after planting and then mulch with a suitable substance. In hot sun and dry weather it might be worth covering the plant with shade netting for a few days to allow it to settle in without stress.

Short-term plantings

Seasonal containers tend to be on the smaller side so can possibly be planted up somewhere else before being moved into their final position. This is useful for hanging baskets and summer bedding pots, as it is easier to plant small plug plants and let them grow a little before putting the whole thing out on display. Again you will need a suitable container, crocks for pots, loam-free compost mixed with slow-release fertiliser, and a range of small plants, preferably a mix of tumbling, trailing plants and taller or bushier ones. If you are using them, water-retaining granules should also be mixed into your compost at this point.

Add a layer of crocks then fill to halfway with compost. Arrange your plants in a suitable design before planting until you get the approximate look you are trying to achieve. Usually the tallest plants go in the centre, and obviously tumbling and trailing plants need to go around the edge so they can drape over, but play around with your design until you are happy. Be generous, but allow just enough room for growth between each plant. Then, and only then, tease out any roots before filling in all gaps with compost mix and firming each plant in gently. Water well and keep shaded and protected until the plants have had a chance to recover and establish.

If weight is an issue polystyrene packing chips can be substituted for crocks.

Routine care of containers

Containers generally need more care than plants in the ground, especially during the growing season. The single biggest issue is likely to be the frequency of watering, followed closely by feeding, as most shop-bought compost is depleted of nutrients within six weeks or even less with heavy watering. In containers plants are unable to access any reserves, unlike plants in the ground, which can hunt out new sources of water and nutrients via their roots, so it is up to you to make up the inevitable shortfall.

Keeping containers trim and tidy is also important as most containers in the garden are a feature and so they should look good at all times. Checking them over for early signs of pests and diseases, regular deadheading and trimming are easy to do at the same time as watering, and if these tasks are undertaken frequently they will hardly take any time at all. Summer bedding flowers especially will continue to flower for much, much longer if deadheaded regularly.

Water the compost, not the plant.

Watering

Deciding how and when to water plants in containers is
a challenge even for experienced gardeners. It is as easy to
overwater as it is to under-water, and it is probably the case that
as many potted and containerised plants have been killed through
overzealous watering as have died through neglect. Very few plants
appreciate having their roots sitting permanently in waterlogged
compost, which prevents vital air from reaching the roots.

Nevertheless it may be the case, depending on position and
weather conditions, that containers need watering up to two or
three times a day. This is probably only necessary with flowering
plants exposed to full sun and drying winds, but it serves as a
reminder that regular checking is essential.

The simplest way to check whether a plant needs water is to
poke a finger deep into the compost to see if there is any moisture
beneath. The fact that the top is dry does not necessarily indicate
that water is required, especially with loam-free compost.

The quickest and most popular way of watering is still the watering can. Always make sure that you water thoroughly, aiming at the compost and avoiding the foliage and flowers. A rose (a watering can head that looks like a shower head) is useful when watering delicate plants that may be bruised and damaged by a strong water flow, and its gentler flow is useful when compost is dry as it will soak in better. Whether you use the watering can's spout or a rose, water steadily until excess water starts to drain through the bottom of the container. The only time this may not indicate that the plant has enough water is if the compost has dried out completely and resists being re-wetted. As dry compost shrinks, water may initially run down the gap created at the side of the pot and straight out at the bottom without doing any good. Check after watering that the compost is evenly moist and repeat if necessary.

It is far better to water thoroughly and leave until dry again than to water a little bit at a time on a more frequent basis. Superficial watering will encourage roots to grow near the surface, leaving them more at risk of drying out in future as well as leading to a build-up of mineral salts in the compost.

For most plants tap water is perfectly adequate. There are some plants, though, that are sensitive to the chemicals in tap water: orchids and carnivorous plants, for example, should only be watered with rain water, easily collected in a water butt. Acid-loving plants, too, may dislike hard tap water with its high mineral content and may be better watered with softer rain water.

For those with more than just a few pots, a hosepipe (though do check for hosepipe bans in the summer months) will save a great deal of time, if not water. An extendable lance will be very useful for watering high-level containers like hanging baskets.

Irrigation systems

Automated watering systems can work well with containers, allowing the busy gardener to concentrate on other tasks and to take the occasional holiday. Seep or porous hoses can be used in bigger containers such as raised beds, but are trickier to use with lots of smaller pots, as they are most water-efficient when laid out in a relatively straight line, along a row of vegetables, say.

A trickle or drip-feed system is a better option. A network of tubes and drip heads can be attached to a low-pressure unit fed by a hosepipe or tap. If not fitted with a timer, water will drip constantly into your pots, which may be wasteful. More expensive timers can be pre-programmed in advance to deliver water exactly when you want it, while simpler devices work only on time, switching off after a set period. Solar-powered timer and drip-feed systems are now also available, which pump more water through the system when it is hot and sunny using the sun's own energy to power themselves. These all need regular cleaning and maintenance to ensure that they work efficiently.

A drip irrigation system can help when you're on holiday.

Reducing water loss

Water is a valuable resource and we should all make every effort to avoid unnecessary wastage. Responsible use begins with collecting and reusing as much water as possible. The more water butts you have room for the better, while watering with grey water (leftover water from baths and washing-up, as long as it does not contain harmful chemicals) is good practice in times of scarcity, especially for those who have no access to water butts. Make sure, too, that any tap and hosepipe connections are in good condition and not leaking, especially if you are using an automated system. Watering early in the morning or later in the evening, at times when evaporation is less of a problem, is sensible, with evening being the best time. This way the plant has the whole of the cooler night to absorb the water it needs. Having said that, a plant that is suffering from water stress should be watered immediately you spot the issue, regardless of the time of day.

Mulching your pots with gravel or bark mulch will also help reduce evaporation and slow down the drying-out process, as will moving smaller pots into the shade in very sunny periods. During times of drought, especially if hosepipe usage has been banned and water is effectively rationed, these small measures may make all the difference.

FEEDING YOUR CONTAINERS

Compost with no extras will only feed your plants for a few weeks, as nutrients are quickly used up by the plant or leached out through watering, especially if the compost is loam-free. Adding slow-release fertilisers at the time of planting can help considerably. These tend to be small pellets that slowly dissolve and release food gradually. Products available from garden centres are nearly all inorganic, which may not suit everyone but will provide the major nutrients, nitrogen, phosphorus and potassium, as well as a range of lesser nutrients depending on the brand. Fortunately organic fertilisers are by their very nature slower-acting than their inorganic counterparts anyway, as they have to be broken down into their constituent parts by soil organisms, which creates a more naturally balanced cycle so there is less need for expensive, branded fertilisers. Chicken manure pellets, or any available granular organic fertiliser, are both good substitutes for inorganic pellets, while seaweed products may be more suitable for those who do not wish to use animal-based products.

Long-term plantings on a bigger scale, like trees and shrubs, can be fertilised with ordinary garden fertilisers, such as blood, fish and bone, too. However, seasonal and short-term planting may need more frequent top-ups from another source.

Liquid fertilisers are much more quick-acting and provide a necessary boost to container plants that have used up their food resources. Containing all essential nutrients, they should be diluted following the instructions and applied to moist soil at the beginning of the growing season and again in midsummer.

In between, diluted foliar feeds can be sprayed on plants that look sick or weak. It is best to use a small sprayer to do this, avoiding any flowers and plants with sensitive leaves. Wait for a dull day as spraying foliar feed on a hot, sunny day can cause leaves to scorch.

Liquid and foliar feeds based on seaweed extracts are now commonly available and many are suitable for organic use. They are especially valuable in supplying a range of trace elements, helping plants remain healthy.

Homemade liquid and foliar feeds are also surprisingly easy to make. The classic home recipe is made using comfrey (*Symphytum officinale*), which is especially rich in potassium and therefore perfect for tomatoes and other flowering and fruiting plants. Simply harvest fresh comfrey leaves, cover with fresh water and steep in a covered waterproof container for around a month. The resulting liquid will be smelly but potent. Water down as required (usually 1 part comfrey concentrate to 15 parts water) and use the remaining leaf sludge as an excellent compost activator. Nettles can be treated the same way, producing a liquid feed that is high in nitrogen and iron and great for leafy plants. It too should be diluted before use.

Homemade liquid feed is easy to make.

There are some plants that may need a more specialist and specific fertiliser to do well. From potato and tomato food for vegetable growing to low-nutrient orchid and cactus compost, most garden centres stock a range that may be helpful for fussy or heavy feeders.

DEADHEADING
AND TRIMMING

It makes sense to keep containers looking good. As they are so often used in areas of high traffic and visibility, there to draw the eye or show off a favourite specimen, they need to be kept neat and tidy. Keeping on top of plant maintenance will also

ensure a longer flowering or better fruiting season for your containerised plants.

Spring tidying for long-term plantings is usually required after winter's travails. Prune out any frost-damaged parts and remove any dead and damaged material before tidying up any straggly or weak shoots. Trimming or pinching out (removing the growing tips by hand) will help make plants bushier and curb any unsightly, straggly growth. Check any ties and supports and replace where necessary.

Deadheading through the growing season will not only improve the appearance of your containers but will in many cases prolong the display of flowers. Plants tend to stop flowering once they have achieved their ultimate goal of producing seed, so removing spent flower heads will encourage them to carry on blooming. This will also reduce the incidence of diseases like grey mould, especially on very soft summer bedding plants like petunias.

Deadheading can usually be done with nothing more than a finger or thumb, pinching out old flowers and their stems back to where they have developed from. Secateurs may sometimes be required for woodier-stemmed plants.

Pinching out old geranium flowers will encourage more blooms and extend the display.

PESTS AND DISEASES

Whether a plant is in the garden or a pot, outside or inside, the same range of diseases, disorders and pests will occur. While it is true that any problems will be more visible on display plants, the extra attention you lavish on your containers should mean that you pick up and spot issues at an early stage. Ideally, ensuring your plants are strong and healthy, with good horticultural practice, is the best method of keeping problems at bay, but prompt action, if you do come across something, will at least prevent any spread from one plant to another and keep damage to a minimum.

There are a number of pests and diseases that you should be able to recognise. Aphids are a problem almost everywhere, but on your precious container displays, they may breed rapidly, especially in areas near the house where birds are less likely to visit. These sap-sucking insects weaken plants, causing distorted and misshapen growing tips especially, and may spread viruses and other diseases. Sometimes an aphid attack will result in black stains on the leaves. This black, sooty substance is a mould that feeds on aphid excretion, known as honeydew, and can prevent photosynthesis as well as looking dirty. Aphids also attract ants, which love to 'farm' them in order to ensure a supply of this honeydew. Although ants rarely do any real damage you may not wish to have them near or even in your house. The easiest way to deal with an aphid attack in the early stages is to rub them off with your fingers or a brush. A good jet of water also works well, as do ladybirds and their larvae if you can catch a few elsewhere and pop them onto your affected plant. If this is not possible, organic soap sprays, applied during a dull period, will desiccate the aphids, or you can, if you wish, use a proprietary pesticide spray to sort your problem out as a last resort.

Slugs and snails can also be a problem, especially as the underside of the pot, damp and moist as it often is, makes an attractive habitat for these creatures. The tell-tale signs are silver slime trails and munched leaves. Check under your pots regularly, and in nearby hiding places, or try any one of a number of methods to keep them away: copper tape, wool pellets, coffee grounds, eggshells or organic slug pellets are just a few suggestions (the list is endless). Avoid the more dangerous inorganic metaldehyde pellets, which could harm pets, children and other wildlife, unless you really feel you must use these.

One pest that is notorious for damaging plants in pots is the vine weevil. The adult beetles, which are grey and just under a centimetre long, cause largely cosmetic damage to leaves, chewing ragged holes and notches out. Although unsightly, there is rarely any long-term damage to the plant, but their larvae are a different story. The adults lay eggs in spring and summer in the compost beneath a plant, which then hatch into white, creamy, curved larvae that eat roots and tissue. The first signs of an attack are slow growth and wilting before the plant collapses and dies completely. They seem to be especially fond of heuchera, but will attack a wide variety of plants from primulas to bigger shrubs, and can even be found in indoor plants.

Good hygiene, clearing away debris that may be sheltering the adults will help, as will regular checking for the larvae, especially when repotting or replacing plants. If you do see signs of unexplained yellowing or wilting, remove the plant completely, checking for signs of the larvae, wash the roots and container and replant in fresh compost. Alternatively, as a precaution or remedy, apply the biological control nematode *Steinernema kraussei*. This natural enemy of the vine weevil is watered onto the compost in late summer when the temperature is between 5° and 21°C (41°–69.8°F), where it will attack and infect any vine weevil larvae, killing them before they cause too much harm. Chemical preparations to deal with vine weevils are also available from garden centres.

Inside greenhouses and houses red spider mite can sometimes be a problem, although it can also live outside in warm conditions. Spider mites are tiny eight-legged insects (not spiders) that cause spotting and mottling of leaves and premature leaf drop, and heavy infestations usually lead to obvious silky fine webs that cover the plant. High humidity created by gently misting the leaves with water can keep them under control, although this is easier to manage inside than out, and a biological control, *Phytoseiulus persimilis*, can be applied in glasshouses. Soap sprays may also have a controlling effect. An increasing resistance to pesticides may limit the efficiency of any chemical spray you might try, so it is best to avoid these if possible.

Other pests that are known to infest container plants – especially but not exclusively under glass – include woolly aphid and mealy bug, and also scale, all of which suck the sap of plants, weakening them and introducing other pathogens. They are visible to the naked eye, and are best cleaned with a finger or brush, or sprayed with horticultural soap before they can develop into a serious infestation.

Finally, more likely problems for plants that require a lot of water or have been overwatered are rots and moulds. Good maintenance and hygiene are key to preventing these problems. Water correctly and remove any dead or damaged material as soon as you see it to reduce the risk of disease. If the problem persists, you may have to replace the plant completely to avoid infecting other plants nearby. Plants infected by a virus should always be removed promptly and burned as there is no remedy.

MAINTENANCE THROUGHOUT THE YEAR

Long-term plantings

Pruning

Long-term container plantings of trees and shrubs as well as cacti and succulents are treated pretty much the same as their garden or glasshouse counterparts. They can be pruned, if required, in exactly the same way, depending on the type of plant. So any dead, diseased and damaged material can be removed at any time of the year, as can crossing branches or any parts that are showing signs of reversion (where a plant chosen for a particular striking characteristic, such as variegated leaves, produces shoots and stems that hark back to its original, less showy parent). More formative or aesthetic pruning should take place at the appropriate time of year for the species.

Generally, during the autumn and winter deciduous and evergreen plants in pots can, by and large, be left to their own devices. Avoid feeding during the colder, dormant season and only water in dry periods, after checking. Spring and summer are the times you will need to pay more care and attention to them.

Repotting

When plants are beginning to outgrow their pot, usually indicated by roots growing through the drainage holes at the bottom, you might want to consider repotting them. This is usually best done just before spring growth starts. Use a pot that is a bit bigger but not too large, as this will mean that the pot holds too much water for the plant size, potentially leading to waterlogging.

*Repot plants
when roots begin to
grow through the
drainage holes.*

As a rough guideline the new pot should be an extra 5cm (2in)
larger around the sides and in height than the current one.

Removing a rootbound plant from its pot can be a bit tricky.
Make sure that it is well watered before trying, and do not
attempt to pull it out by its leaves. Instead tip the pot on its side
and tap gently with a trowel, or squeeze if flexible enough, before
gently working out the plant while holding on to the strongest
stem or trunk. If all else fails you may have to cut apart or smash
the pot. Once the plant has been removed, try to tease out the
roots so that they will spread better when potted on. Sometimes a
hand-fork may help you gain purchase on an especially tangled
rootball, but fortunately roots are generally pretty robust. Large
plants may eventually get so big that repotting is no longer a
viable option, but they can be transferred to the garden where
possible, top-dressed (where the top layer of old compost is
scraped away and replaced with fresh) or root-pruned.

Short-term plantings

As these tend to be more seasonal and will be removed when finished or replaced, there is rarely a need to worry about pruning or repotting. Regular watering, feeding, condition-checking and deadheading, possibly with a light trim, are all that will be required until the display is finished, although poor, spent or diseased plants can be swapped for better ones at any time with relative ease if necessary.

Holidays and absences

Most of us will spend part of the year away from our pots and containers for one reason or another. This can cause no end of angst unless you happen to be lucky enough to have a reliable friend, neighbour or relative to help out. Even if you do, you should still make it as easy as possible for them to keep your pots in good condition with minimum fuss.

The main issue with containers left for any length of time is clearly water. To minimise water loss through evaporation try to move all containers into the shadiest place you have and group them all together. Capillary matting placed underneath, connected to a water reservoir, is one option, or a simple drip-feed system on a timer may be a worthwhile investment if you travel a lot. Failing that, a container filled with water and sand or gravel placed underneath your pots may be enough to keep them moist for short periods of time, so the plants do not become waterlogged.

If you do return and find your plants on their last legs, do not despair. Try immersing them in a bucket of water for 30 minutes or so to ensure that the dried-out compost is completely wet and see if they recover. Be patient with your plants and see what happens for a few weeks before giving up.

Winter protection

Pots and containers may need extra protection in periods of extreme cold as compost and roots can easily become frozen. For Mediterranean and 'tropical' plants this could be a real problem. If possible move your least hardy pots somewhere frost-free such as a glasshouse or porch, or wrap them in fleece or other insulating material during cold snaps. Make sure the pots are wrapped too, in hessian or plastic bubble wrap to keep frost from delicate roots. This may also help prevent vulnerable pots from cracking in frost. Spring too can bring sharp and unexpected frosts, so only dispense with any protection when you are sure that all danger of frost has passed.

There are a few other factors to consider when it comes to maintenance through the year. Grouping containers together will probably lead to dirt and debris getting trapped around the bases, which ideally should be swept regularly to prevent the build-up of pests or diseases. Containers of plants on hard surfaces may also cause staining and algae growth so jet washing or careful use of an algae remover or patio cleaner may be required at some point. Using feet, wheels or some sort of stand for your pots may help reduce this issue.

Wrapping vulnerable plants in fleece will help protect them from frost.

OUTDOOR
POTS

PERMANENT TREES, SHRUBS, CLIMBERS AND STANDARDS

A tree or shrub in a pot can lend an air of maturity to any space and is often a good choice for the centrepiece of a mixed display, giving year-round interest and structure even if the rest of the planting is seasonal and short-lived. They also make excellent specimen or feature plants, and fit well with formal and architectural designs.

Choose plants in good condition for planting as poor specimens may not cope well with the artificial conditions. The ideal tree or shrub should have a good all-round structure, be free of any disease or pests, and should not be potbound or have roots showing through the drainage holes. Pot-grown plants are probably better than bare root, being more stable and easier to plant.

Planting trees

Make sure that the pot or container for a tree is both large enough and stable enough to cope with the top growth that most trees are likely to produce. Broad-bottomed planters, like the Versailles planter or wooden barrels, are perfect, but anything that has weight, width and depth will do. Unlike smaller plantings, trees need containers that are much larger than the rootball in order to develop anchoring roots and grow successfully.

A container at least one and a half times the depth of the rootball and as wide as around a quarter of the tree's height should suffice.

Trees are best planted in loam-based compost with added slow-release fertiliser and using crocks for drainage. It is also worth staking them, as you would do with any planted tree, preferably with something sturdy enough to be left permanently in place to help your tree withstand wind. A single stake is usually all that will be required, tall enough to come up to the head of the tree and kept in place with adjustable ties that will cope with the ever-expanding girth of the growing trunk. Check regularly and make sure that the ties are not rubbing off the bark and biting into the tree trunk. It is important to loosen them before damage occurs as the wounds can open the way for infection from pathogens, and trees will often callus over these wounds and the ties as a protection, making them difficult to adjust later or remove. Stakes vary from long canes to wrought-iron metalwork depending on your budget and style. Mulching with bark mulch or gravel will help to retain valuable moisture.

Trees that do well in pots include acers, birches and cordylines, citrus (which will need bringing indoors in winter), and bay, olive and loquat in sheltered locations, as well as other fruit trees like apples, pears, cherries and plums on small rootstocks. Dwarf conifers are also a good choice and look especially good in symmetrical designs, where their strong, defined shapes and textures will stand out while requiring little attention other than a good watering regime.

Trees are best planted in large pots to allow room for their roots to grow.

There are a number of palms too that look fantastic in pots and will give your patio or garden a more exotic feel without too much effort. *Chamaerops humilis*, the dwarf fan palm, is a good choice as it is bushy rather than tall, while *Trachycarpus wagnerianus*, the dwarf chusan palm, will withstand exposure to wind better than most palms. Blue palms are also very attractive, although a little less hardy. In sheltered locations *Butia capitata* (jelly palm) or the silvery-blue form of the dwarf fan palm can really make a strong statement.

Root pruning

As trees get bigger it becomes impractical to find larger and larger pots for them. If manageable you may be able to root-prune your tree to keep it compact and slow its growth rate. Regular root-pruning is an essential activity in bonsai maintenance, and is often undertaken by commercial tree surgeons so you should not worry that you might seriously harm the tree unless you are very unlucky.

Once the tree is removed from the pot, always the most difficult part, the bottom third to half of the rootball can be cut away. Tease out and prune some of the long, winding roots to encourage new, straighter roots to spread before replanting in fresh compost. If you cannot remove the tree completely it may be possible to use a trenching shovel or sharp border spade to gradually work around the edge and slice at an angle underneath, thus separating much of the lower rootball in order to lift the tree out. It is hard, however, to be sure how much root you are cutting away, so this is best used only as a last resort, if the tree is really looking unhealthy and in danger of dying from crowded roots.

Top pruning

Early pruning of a container tree should concentrate on creating a good, balanced shape to ensure that as it grows it does not become lopsided and therefore more likely to tip over. Once you have achieved this follow the pruning guidelines for the tree in question as if it was in the garden. This may be no pruning at all, or very little. Apple trees in pots, for example, will need exactly the same pruning regime as their bigger cousins in the garden to fruit well.

Shrubs

There are plenty of shrubs that will happily grow successfully in containers. For those with smaller garden spaces, a shrub or a collection of shrubs can fulfil the same role as a tree, providing backbone and structure to more ephemeral displays, but many also make a wonderful statement when planted alone or in series.

The list of suitable shrubs for containers has to begin with the classic evergreen, box, most often seen clipped formally into geometric shapes. Topiary is almost a must in formal gardens, the shapes only limited by your imagination and skill with the shears. Even simple shapes, such as balls, cones and pyramids, can look elegant and refined and make a great focal point or centrepiece, while a symmetrical series or line of potted topiary will bring a polished, stylised sense of control to your garden space. If you are not confident in your ability to shape topiary from scratch, most basic shapes are now commonly available to buy. Even in predominantly informal gardens, clipped box may be just the thing to highlight and reinforce the blowsiness elsewhere. Counterpoint through contrast is a classic design technique.

A similar effect can be achieved with other shrubs, too. Skimmias, hebes and lavender all look good as a repetitive motif and may be more suitable in specific conditions. Lavender, for example, is the perfect choice for a hot, sunny area such as a south-facing balcony or a hot patio, and requires less attention than clipped box. Its fragrance is also an important bonus.

There is a whole range of shrubs that have more specific environmental requirements and may have to be grown in containers for purely practical reasons. Shrubs that would be unable to cope with cold winter conditions can be moved under glass in their planters when the season turns and then brought back out on display in warmer months. *Brugmansia*, commonly known as angel's trumpets, oleanders, *Lantana camara* (yellow sage), *Tibouchina* and the less hardy fuchsias are all fabulous sub-tropical shrubs that will bring an exotic feel and a mass of flowers to your garden space in the summer, and it is certainly a lot easier and less risky to keep plants like these in movable pots than trying to transplant them into the garden each year.

Other shrubs may simply prefer soil conditions that you cannot provide elsewhere. Unless you have naturally acid soil, azaleas, camellias, rhododendrons and many heathers will not do well in chalky garden soil, even with your most assiduous attention. The uphill battle of constantly adding ericaceous matter and food to soil is rarely effective, and most acid-loving plants in the wrong type of soil will inevitably become weaker over time or even die. Ericaceous compost in pots, with added slow-release ericaceous fertiliser, will suit acid-loving plants perfectly. Mulch ericaceous pots with bark mulch, leaf mould or pine needles rather than gravel, which may contain traces of lime.

Generally, having containers of specialised compost mixes can greatly increase the diversity of your planting schemes. For plants that like dry, free-draining conditions, such as yuccas and agaves, add sand and gravel, while for those that appreciate damp, moist soil add a higher proportion of organic matter such as leaf mould or homemade compost, which will hold more water. As long as you position the pots in the right place your favourite plants should flourish.

Climbers

Climbers can be grown very successfully in pots as long as some sort of support is provided. The most usual form is trellis. Specialist shapes perfectly designed for container growing are available with legs that can be sunk into the compost for extra stability. These should be placed into the pot at the back while you are filling up with compost and firmed in as you go. Once you have added your climbing plant tie in any main shoots and water well. Ideally it is better to plant in position, as moving a trellis can be tricky. It is also worth fixing the trellis to a wall or fence wherever possible as most climbers are naturally top heavy and dense so may be caught in high winds. For this reason, too, a sheltered position is a good idea. Plants that grow well up trellis include clematis and jasmine. Annual climbers like sweet peas and runner beans (which were originally brought to this country for their decorative flowers) can also be grown up cane or stick wigwams for an informal, riotously joyful look. Less hardy climbers, like their shrub counterparts, can also be grown in containers so they can be moved inside in winter. Bougainvillea, stephanotis and *Trachelospermum* (confederate jasmine) are all delightfully exotic specimens that will be happy in a warm, sheltered position for the summer season.

Ivy is the most common climber found in planting schemes. Its decorative, heart-shaped leaves and climbing or tumbling habit make it a classic in many designs, filling bare patches beautifully while not overwhelming any other planting, but it can also be a feature in its own right or provide the linking theme and

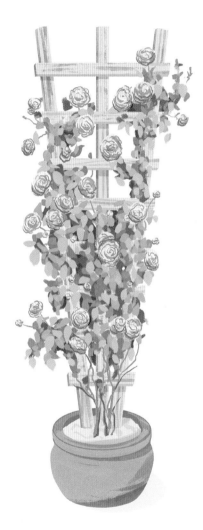

a sense of continuity between pots planted with a variety of arrangements.

Standards

There are a number of trees, shrubs and woody-stemmed climbers that can be grown as standards, trained and pruned into a tree-like shape. The length of the trunk and the lollipop of leaves and flowers at the top mean that standards should always be grown in wide, heavy pots for stability. Training a plant into a standard is not only aesthetically pleasing but practical; using up less space at ground level and allowing more light to reach any planting underneath. Creating a standard, unfortunately, is not simply a matter of cutting

Always provide sturdy support for climbers in a pot.

Growing a tree or shrub standard requires patience, but the results are worth it.

off all the lower growth. It may take up to five years to train a plant into a standard, gradually developing a strong, vigorous main stem to the right height and pruning out sideshoots during several winters before allowing the head to expand by tip pruning to ensure plenty of bushy growth. Even the most vigorous of climbers such as wisteria can be kept in check with a bit of care and a firm hand.

PERENNIALS, ANNUALS AND BIENNIALS

Perennials

Traditionally perennials grown in containers are the more tender, exotic varieties such as pelargoniums (often commonly referred to as geraniums), which are sometimes treated as annuals to minimise the effort of protecting them through winter. There are many other plants that fall into this category. As well as the traditional geraniums, scented geraniums make a fine display, although they may not survive the winter. Placing them beside sunny paths will help release their scent as you brush past them. *Calceolaria* (slipper flower), *Tradescantia*, *Osteospermum* and *Arctotis* also fit in well with bright summer schemes, while *Helichrysum* (everlasting flower), ostensibly bought as an annual pot filler, will often survive through a mild winter.

There is no reason, though, why hardier perennials cannot also be grown in pots. *Heuchera* make great container subjects, with a wide variety of colours available from lime green to plum, and they work well with colourful annuals and bedding plants. You could also try astilbes, ferns and hostas in shady areas for interesting form and texture, while more traditional border plants like the shorter phlox or alchemilla and primulas suit informal garden schemes. You can use *Ajuga reptans* (bugle) to disguise any bare compost, allowing one or two statement plants to rise up, if ivy is not to your taste. The purple versions are excellent as a foil for silver foliage and blue and white flowers.

There is also a whole range of grasses, which can look wonderful in a container either with or without other plants. The smaller grasses, such as blue *Festuca* (tufted fescue), *Carex* (remote sedge) and the beautiful black lily grass offer a delightful contrast, with their upright spikes, to more delicate, spreading flowering plants, while the larger ones look fabulously stylish in longer, taller pots. *Pennisetum* (fountain grass), *Miscanthus* and *Deschampsia* (wavy hair grass), for example, look like fluffy, elegant fountains and make great statement plants.

There are many other, larger perennials with distinct architectural forms that work well as statement plants, and also as stand-alone features, especially in areas of hard landscaping. Yucca, phormiums (which come in a wide variety of colours), bamboo and astelia will all add style to a patio, balcony or roof garden.

Annuals and biennials

As a rule when we think about plants in pots it is often the bright summer displays that come to mind first. Despite the fact that many of these plants are actually half-hardy perennials, we usually find it easier to buy and plant them fresh each year, when any chance of frost has passed. Spring in the garden centre is when shelves fill with a variety of summer bedding plants, with numerous cultivars on offer. Lobelia, petunias, marigolds, bedding dahlias, nicotiana and pelargoniums are just some of the classic summer plants on offer, alongside plants that are less well-known but make for wonderful hanging baskets or planters. Many can also be grown from seed, the more tender exotic plants requiring heat to get started, but there are plenty of annuals that can be sown directly into pots, such as calendula, and a range of easy-to-grow native flowers, especially useful for attracting wildlife and pollinators. There are fewer varieties of winter annuals, but they should not be ignored. Pansies and violas are widely available, as are bedding primulas and primroses, and there are always spring-flowering biennials such as wallflowers that can bring colour to your displays, especially in combination with bulbs.

Relative depths for planting daffodils, hyacinths and tulips for a spring display.

SEASONAL DISPLAYS

One of the great advantages of growing plants in pots and containers is the possibility of change and variety. In spring pots of bulbs take centre stage, and once their flowering is over they can be tucked away out of sight to perform the ugly act of dying off without offence. They can then be replaced with bright summer bedding, trailing plants, scented herbs, summer-flowering annuals and perennials, and with hanging baskets and window boxes full of colour. These too can be removed once they look tired, leaving the autumn colours and berries of potted shrubs and trees. Acers and grasses are often the stars of autumn, while in winter evergreens and scented winter-flowering shrubs will still provide welcome interest even on the grimmest of days.

It takes some effort to manage this endless change and diversity, but it is not impossible. Depending on your lifestyle and the time you have, you may decide to limit yourself to just one or two seasonal effects or to plant pots that will work over more than one season. However, it is better to have one big,

fantastic pot containing a statement plant like a silver birch, a bamboo or a spiky agave than to litter your garden space with unwanted, mismatched pots of plants that have nothing in common and simply look uncared for.

Spring bulb pots are easy to plant and take up relatively little space. By planting a variety of bulbs that flower at slightly different times you can have a longer flowering season. Try planting combinations of snowdrops, hyacinths, narcissus and tulips in one pot for a display that will last from late January to May. Add pansies or violas, perennial daisies and forget-me-nots, or an evergreen shrub such as skimmia, to give extra interest.

In summer the availability of plants for pots increases dramatically. Mixed arrangements made up of a central feature plant such as a fuchsia, surrounded by bushy and tumbling, trailing plants always look wonderful. If you buy your plants early in the season you will possibly have to protect them from any late frost for a while, but you can also take the opportunity to keep pinching out the growing tips so that they branch more and become bushier as they develop. This will not only cover the compost better but will encourage more flowers to form.

Before diving into planting any container, place your plants on top of the compost while still in their pots and move them around until you are happy with the look. This prevents any harm coming to exposed plant roots by repeatedly rearranging them. Good summer combinations include purple petunias and orange daisies perhaps with a lime green heuchera, or dwarf cannas, sedums and trailing begonias for a hot, tropical look. Gentler combinations of silver, pink and white suit cottage and informal gardens very well. Add a touch of blue to give an extra seaside-inspired touch.

Plant a variety of spring bulbs to extend the flowering display.

Sometimes simple arrangements can have just as much impact. A row of terracotta pots, perhaps up a set of steps, planted with nothing but red geraniums takes up very little space but will instantly invoke a certain continental *je ne sais quoi*, as will window boxes overflowing with ivy-leaved geraniums, staple of alpine chalets in summer and Parisian apartments.

Growing similar plants together in collections also works well. Mixed herb pots or edible flowers look and taste delicious and make perfect summer displays. Or grow annuals and grasses that will attract pollinators and other insects. Pots for wildlife may not have the wow factor of showy summer bedding, but the pleasure of watching all the insect activity may more than make up for this. Children especially, now that they are so well informed at school about the planet's ecology, often enjoy planting and monitoring wildlife-friendly pots.

Growing any kind of plants in pots is a great way of introducing children to gardening, giving them a manageable project to gently stretch their imaginations, whether it be growing mini veg or creating landscapes that dinosaurs or pixies can wander through.

Containers can be practical as well as eye-catching.

Hanging baskets are a classic way of displaying plants.

HANGING BASKETS
AND WINDOW BOXES

A typical hanging basket is light, usually made of plastic-coated wire, although baskets woven from fibre are increasingly popular. They are normally lined with coir, paper or wool, although many people choose to make their own liners using black plastic, which is easier to fit to shape but needs to be well hidden with plants to look good. Whatever they are made from, they are, for many people, the quintessential summer container display.

What matters more than the style and type is the safety of the fixing as a fully laden basket can be surprisingly weighty and potentially dangerous to passers-by. Use hanging baskets only if you can ensure that fixings are secure. A bracket securely attached to a strong wall or structure is the usual method, though half-moon baskets with a flat back attached to the wall are another, probably safer option.

Hanging baskets are usually planted with tiers of bushy and trailing plants that drape over and down from planting holes, and are designed to be seen from every direction. To plant, rest the basket on a bucket for stability, and fit and adjust any liner so it does not overhang the rim. If there are no pre-cut holes use a craft knife to cut staggered tiers of slits about 5cm (2in) wide in the side of the liner before filling up to the bottom tier with a good-quality potting compost mixed with slow-release fertiliser and water-retaining granules. Use small plug plants rather than larger pot specimens, as you will have to feed plants through the holes without damaging the rootball too much. Wrap the green part of each plant in cardboard or plastic to make a kind of protective sleeve before feeding this through the planting slit from the inside until only the rootball is sitting on compost, removing the protection from the plant when you have finished. Keep working round the basket, adding plants and filling with compost before adding a last layer of trailing or lax plants at the top and a slightly bushier one in the middle. Ivy, petunias, lobelia, *Dichondra* and verbena all work well, or you could choose edible plants like tumbling tomatoes and strawberries to ring the changes. Trailing plants can be angled when planting to encourage them to grow in the right direction. Once all the planting is complete, water well and leave in a protected place to establish before displaying when all chance of frost has passed.

Maintaining hanging baskets can be a challenge due to their height but a long lance attachment for a hosepipe will help with watering. Alternatively you can buy pulley systems that allow you to drop the height in order to water, feed and deadhead. Otherwise a stepladder will probably be required.

Window boxes too should be fixed securely, as wind and clumsiness can easily knock them off with potentially disastrous results. Add crocks for drainage before filling two-thirds of the way up with good potting compost. Then start adding your plants. Normally trailing plants are planted at the front and bushier, more structured plants at the back, but your choice of plants will also be dependent on the amount of light your boxes will receive.

More formal window boxes tend to have evergreens like box and ivy, while South African daisies (*Osteospermum*) or dwarf sunflowers look fabulous in a sunny position. A collection of the more decorative herbs like thyme and chives can also work beautifully.

Window boxes are ideal for those with limited space.

A mini pond can be a wonderful feature.

WATER GARDEN CONTAINERS

A pond is a wonderful feature in a garden but not always practical if space is limited or young children are around. You can still bring the sense of tranquillity and reflection that only water can offer by creating a mini pond in a container, even in a small space. If you pick your plants wisely, a relatively shallow container can play host to a variety of interesting combinations. Usually, though, a deeper container is a better choice and will allow for a wider variety of planting.

The most common choice for a mini pond in a container is the half-barrel, but any watertight container with a good surface area can be used. Small ponds like this are best placed in part sun, somewhere sheltered but away from trees that will drop their leaves in autumn. They need to be on a level surface for obvious reasons.

Block off any drainage holes in new half-barrels by gluing pebbles over the holes or sealing with an appropriate product, before soaking the barrel in water thoroughly to fully expand the slats. This will ensure it remains watertight. Older barrels, or those that will not hold water properly, can be lined with pond liner first. Add a layer of gravel at the bottom before filling just over halfway with water.

Water plants are usually bought in special plastic mesh containers unless they have arrived through the post. To make your own, take a small plastic mesh basket lined with sacking before filling with garden soil and adding your water plant. Always top dress with gravel to stop the soil washing out.

Deep-water plants like waterlilies can probably be lowered directly onto the bottom of the pond, while stacked bricks and stones can be used to raise the height of baskets and containers of marginal plants, those that would normally live on the edge of a river or lake. This group of plants includes rushes, water forget-me-not, sweet flag and the wonderful bulrush. Make sure too that you add an oxygenating plant, one that is not invasive, to keep the water healthy. Floating aquatic plants, such as water lettuce and water hyacinth, can also be added. Keep an eye on their spread and remove some if they are completely covering the water surface. Some partial coverage is good though as it helps to prevent algal growth.

In a standard half-barrel, which holds about 50 litres (11 gallons) of water, there should be room for one pygmy waterlily, two to three marginal plants, at least one oxygenator and one floating aquatic.

Gently top up your barrel with water if necessary and adjust the bricks and stones until each plant is just reaching the top of the water. In winter you might need to protect your barrel from the cold or remove any plants that are not hardy. If you have small children wire mesh can be tacked over the top for safety reasons.

There are plenty of other containers that can fulfil the same function as a half-barrel. Anything that is watertight or can be made so, such as old water troughs, glazed ceramic planters, even plastic storage containers or upside-down dustbin lids (which may need disguising or burying into soil) can become short-term or long-term ponds. It is easy to add a solar-powered fountain if you have enough water in your container to feed the pump, or you could try dyeing the water with food colouring for effect without causing any harm to plants or wildlife. Black water is highly fashionable and appears in many modern designs as it reflects everything that is going on above it. A small and stylish temporary pond is easily created with nothing more than a shallow container, a few drops of black food colouring and a suitable statement plant such as a small-leaved gunnera or a calla lily.

Use gravel and gritty compost for growing succulents.

DRY CONTAINERS

Cacti, succulents and other similar plants, like many alpines, make perfect specimens for container growing. Their relatively small size and low maintenance requirements make them easy to care for as long as they are given the right environmental conditions to begin with. These are all plants that have evolved to cope with poor, rocky soil and less water than usual, so if time is an issue, or you travel a lot, this may be your answer.

The most critical factor in successfully growing these drought-resistant plants is sharp drainage.

Any container you use must have good drainage holes to ensure excess water drains away quickly. Wide, shallow terracotta pots with four or five holes are excellent as are old ceramic sinks, possibly with extra drilled holes.

Before planting make sure that there is a good deep layer, about a third of the total container depth, of crocks and gravel at the base before filling up with gritty, sandy compost and planting into it. Top dressing with further grit is also usual, and some people like to add decorative pebbles or stones for effect. Cacti and succulents are plants that often work well in groups, with taller column types mixing with spreading, ground-hugging plants. Most plants like this tolerate and even enjoy plenty of sun and heat, but check before you mix plants up in the same container as there are a few that prefer shade or slightly cooler conditions. Generally, though, a warm, dry position is preferred. Water only when dry, but do water thoroughly when you do, and rest them during the colder winter months with protection from frost and very wet weather.

There are a wide range of succulents and cacti that will do well in containers, pots and troughs. Easy plants include houseleeks, *Echeveria*, aloes and aeoniums, while numerous cacti can be tried. Most small alpines are also suitable, and an alpine trough is a classic of many people's gardens. In most cases alpines like slightly richer soil than succulents and cacti, so adjust your compost mix accordingly.

For a bigger, stronger statement, large single succulents in big pots can look fabulous. Century plant (*Agave americana*), for example, with its spiky, dramatic leaves, will thrive in a sunny position and makes an excellent focal point. It has a number of variegated forms that are very sought-after.

Runner beans make a jolly summer display.

'GROW YOUR OWN'
IN CONTAINERS

A traditional edible garden can take up quite a bit of space, especially those that are planted with a wide variety of produce or are rotated on a yearly basis, to help minimise pests and diseases. For those that do not have the advantage of a spare piece of land or who do not wish to give over such a large part of their garden for such utilitarian purposes, there are still ways to have tasty crops using up much less space. Even a kitchen windowsill can become a mini allotment or herb garden.

There is a resurgence in growing your own, as people begin to question the quality and environmental impact of buying produce that may have been flown in from other parts of the world or stored for a lengthy period of time. The chemicals that are sprayed on vegetables and fruit, the conditions they are grown in and that people have to work in, the constant monotony of availability and unseasonality, the environmental damage and effect on wildlife: these are all concerns for many people who have turned to their own resources to compensate. In urban areas space might always be an issue, but imagination can overcome most problems and although city dwellers may not be able to become completely self-sufficient, there is always a way to grow something yourself.

What and how you grow something is really dependent on the environment you have at your disposal. Light can be a real issue in built-up cities, for example, so vegetables that need plenty of sun to ripen, such as tomatoes, aubergines and courgettes, may not be sensible on a north-facing patio. Vegetables that need a long period of time to mature, like parsnips, or are naturally hungry for nutrients, such as cabbages, are also probably not the best option, but that still leaves a wide variety of crops to grow and harvest.

Most fruit and vegetables need rich soil or compost to grow well and produce a useful harvest, and they all need a regular and consistent supply of water. The compost found in good grow bags is ideal, with extra fertiliser top-ups later on in the season. Regular foliar feeding is especially beneficial. If you use ordinary compost try adding well-rotted compost along with some sand to ensure that it remains well aerated even with the extra watering you may have to give it.

Small pots and containers

There are plenty of quick-maturing, compact crops that can be grown in relatively small pots. Lettuce, radishes and baby beetroot take very little time to grow and are anyway best eaten when young. Leafy vegetables such as spinach, leaf beet and rocket leaves can be sown in containers as small as empty food cans, easily replaced as soon as they start to age and mature. Successional sowing – sowing small amounts regularly and often – is the standard way of ensuring a constant supply of fresh produce and is even easier if you use containers. Sow a new small pot every couple of weeks and you will always have a supply of tasty young crops to look forward to. Pots of herbs too, such as basil, coriander, parsley and chives, can be sown successionally in small pots. Kept on the windowsill or close to the door onto your outdoor space, these will ensure a fresh supply that is easy to get at quickly and more likely, therefore, to be utilised. Sprouts, shoots and microgreens, the smallest possible edible plants, are sown in nothing more than a shallow tray or an old fruit punnet containing a thin layer of compost. Radish, cress, spinach, mustard, lettuce and small beans are all popular and very good for you. With a little more depth of soil peas can be germinated and the delicate, elegant shoots cropped and eaten as a garnish.

If you are at all foodie, you might also want to grow some small pots of edible flowers, like violets and heartsease, along with any herbs, as these look rather lovely garnishing fine dishes.

Larger containers

Larger, deeper pots will give you a much greater range of vegetables and fruits. Today there are plenty of dwarf or patio varieties of classic garden produce easily grown from seed or available from a good garden centre. Broad beans, peas, bush tomatoes, aubergines and all manner of crops now come in miniature, having been bred specially for container growing and smaller garden spaces. Longer pots, too, can be used successfully to grow root crops like carrots and leeks. Using fine, stone-free potting compost often means that they grow straighter and longer than their garden counterparts, and in fact exhibition growers often grow their prize exhibits exactly this way to achieve their record-breaking results. Potatoes and cordon tomatoes (the taller varieties) are also possible but will need plenty of container space to flourish. Even full-sized runner beans can be grown successfully in a container with a cane tripod support as long as they have enough root space. Any container you use for climbing vegetables should be deep and wide enough to be stable, whatever the weather.

Keep all vegetable pots well watered and provide plenty of extra food as necessary. As a rule of thumb, the bigger the vegetable plant the hungrier it is likely to be. Comfrey liquid, seaweed or proprietary fertiliser should all be applied at a suitable rate throughout the growing season.

Growing potatoes

Potatoes in pots can be a revelation. You may not get a huge crop but the potatoes you do produce will be delicious and fresh as they seem to grow quicker this way. There are plenty of early and second early varieties to try. New and salad varieties as well as waxy-skinned potatoes do best in pots, rather than the larger maincrops, and there are now even varieties to grow for eating at Christmas. Try 'Charlotte', 'Maris Peer' or 'International Kidney' (the potato grown in Jersey) or look out for specialities.

If aesthetics are not an issue, large sturdy bags or even stacks of old tyres can be used, but a decent-sized pot will still produce a useful crop. Good compost is essential. Begin by filling the pot by a third before placing a few seed potatoes on top and covering lightly with compost. Water well and frequently and protect if frost threatens. As the plants grow add more compost and granular fertiliser to just cover the new growth each time until you reach the top of the container. Your crop should be ready between 12 and 16 weeks from planting, depending on the variety. You can easily harvest just the amount you need for one meal and leave the rest undisturbed.

Grow a fabulous crop of potatoes using old tyres.

Grow bags and raised beds

Grow bags are often sold specifically for growing vegetables, especially tomatoes, and can be useful in small, hard-landscaped spaces as well as practical in glasshouses, which may have hard floors or borders that are known to contain pathogens. Always buy the best quality that you can afford as the cheaper ones tend to be too thin to allow good root growth. They will need drainage holes, but to avoid infection and stagnation cut these along the sides of the base and not underneath. Although the plastic bag will prevent water evaporating it will also heat up rather more than terracotta or ceramic, which may affect the plant roots somewhat, so, if possible, cover with straw, leaves or planks to reduce direct heat from the sun. There are now products on the market as well which will hide your grow bag more stylishly if you want to splash out.

Where possible it might be better to buy or build a raised bed. This can be extremely useful if you have problems bending down as it can be built to a suitably comfortable height to work on. The extra depth of compost too will suit just about every vegetable and generally improve their performance.

Raised beds laid directly on top of the ground are now a staple of many modern vegetable patches, although the tradition dates back to the medieval period, but the same advantages apply if you build a box with a base as long as it is deep enough to support proper root growth. You can plant much more closely and grow more in a raised bed than you can do with straight line planting and there are fewer pest and disease problems to contend with, as the compost within should be sterile and free from any long-lasting soil pathogens. The extra height also means warmer soil, giving you a longer growing season.

Grow more in a small space by subdividing your beds.

It is relatively easy to make your own raised beds out of timber, or ready-made kits in wood or plastic can be bought. There is nothing to prevent you from attaching wheels to your boxes so they can be pushed around to make the most of environmental conditions. For something more substantial and permanent, bricks and stones are a possibility.

Any containers made of timber are likely to rot as a result of the near-constant exposure to moisture, so do make sure you treat them with a preservative that will not leach dangerous chemicals into your compost and thence into your vegetables. A plastic inner lining is also a good idea and will extend the lifespan of your box by a number of years.

The actual size of a raised bed or box is dependent on both the amount of space available and the reach of the gardener as climbing up to reach over is not a wise idea. Usually boxes of 1 sq m (10¾ sq ft) are recommended but they can be smaller or larger if this suits better.

Making the most of what space you have can be an exciting and challenging prospect. One method is to further divide the space into smaller squares, planting each one with a different vegetable. Known as square foot gardening, this is a method developed in America in the 1970s and remains a popular way to use the space sensibly. However, you may wish to simply fill with your favourites or make it more or less decorative.

Growing fruit

Strawberries make excellent container plants. In the right sort of pot or even a hanging basket the ripe fruit can hang beautifully, free from dirt and the worst of slug attacks. In flower they are also very pretty and so may well fit in with decorative pots.

Bush fruit, too, can work well in containers. Blackcurrants, redcurrants, gooseberries (best kept out of the way as they are prickly) and even blueberries in acidic compost will give up their bounty merrily as long as you take good care of them and keep them well watered and fed. Raspberries are a little trickier only in that they need a slightly bigger pot to allow for their tendency to throw up new shoots a little way from the original canes, and you should try to choose shorter-growing varieties. Hybrid berries too will work, given some sort of frame to tie the long, leggy shoots in. Look for thornless varieties to make picking easier.

If you want to try your hand at fruit trees there is now a wide range of varieties on dwarfing rootstocks. Apples, pears, plums, cherries, nectarines and peaches can all be bought this way, making them a suitable size for container growing. You may want to take into consideration, though, that the higher the container, the higher the final crop of the tree will be, so err on the safe side if you do not want to get the stepladder out. Apple trees, at least, can sometimes be found grown on extremely dwarfing rootstocks that should only ever grow to around 1.2m (4ft), useful in really small spaces.

Special strawberry pots will produce a good crop in a small space.

INDOOR
POTS

INDOOR CONTAINERS

Increasingly, growing plants indoors is becoming a more familiar pastime. Where once a variety of houseplants would be found decorating 'parlours' and bathroom windowsills, today's indoor plants are as varied and interesting as the plants we see outdoors. From modern designs that integrate trees and shrubs into the very fabric of an interior to kitchen windowsill allotments, more and more of us have turned to green decoration to mitigate the harshness of modern life and the vagaries of the weather. If getting out into the garden is not possible every day, then many of us are more than happy to bring it inside.

There are many different ways to enjoy and use indoor plants. A single table decoration may be enough for someone busy with other things, or a fan of modernism – perhaps an easy-to-care-for bromeliad with a strong, defined shape. Kitchens can be crammed with growing produce for those who love cooking, conservatories filled with a lush selection of tropical-looking foliage and flowers, and spare rooms and shelves decorated with specialist collections. All need to be kept in containers of some sort or another – and all need greater or lesser maintenance, just like plants outside.

Temperature and light are the two most important considerations when it comes to growing plants indoors. Houses are warmer throughout the year than the outside and the temperature tends to vary less on a day-to-day basis. However it may drop considerably at night if the heating is switched off, something that can have an impact on more tropical plants used

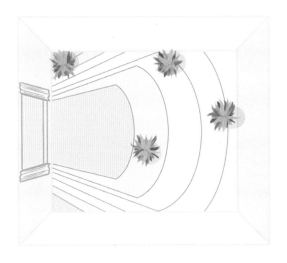

Internal light levels vary depending on a room's layout.

to higher temperatures. Windowsills too are not necessarily providers of the perfect environment, despite many plants ending up there, as proximity to cold glass, draughts and hot radiators can all cause harm.

Light is another big issue since, in the majority of cases, the rooms we live in only have windows on one or two sides. Rarely do houseplants receive light from all around and above. Not only this, but the further away a plant is from the window the less light it receives. The area of a room with windows at the opposite end may be receiving as little as 20 per cent of the total natural light. All plants need light in some form or another or they will die. In low light they quickly become weak and pale, or worse, become etiolated, where stems stretch towards the nearest light and get spindly and drawn out. Adequate light for the species you have chosen is always critical to long-term success. There are also many plants that have a tendency to grow in the direction of light, whatever the levels they prefer, and this can cause long-term lop-sidedness. Turn such plants a little each day, or whenever you water, to prevent this.

On the whole most plants prefer bright light rather than direct sunlight, especially when it is magnified through glass. In the brightest, sunniest places, cacti, succulents and pelargoniums are a sensible choice, as are plants with grey or woolly leaves. Orchids and foliage plants like fan plant (*Begonia rex*) prefer indirect light, slightly filtered, which may be an excuse to bring out the net curtains, while the darkest parts of your room will be tolerated by ivy, most ferns and tough-leaved jungle plants. Ferns, too, do well in bathrooms, where the extra humidity is appreciated.

Fortunately there are one or two houseplants that are extremely tolerant in almost every situation. Aspidistras and mother-in-law's tongue (*Sansevieria trifasciata*) are long-suffering staples in many homes, as is the almost infamous spider plant. Forced bulbs, too, can be placed just about anywhere while in flower as long as you move them to more suitable conditions during the rest of their growing period.

Watering

Plants indoors are totally reliant on the water you supply, meaning that even more care needs to be taken when looking after them. Overwatering is as much of a problem as under-watering as many houseplants are sold precisely because they are easy-care, which effectively translates as tolerant of a little neglect and not requiring too much in the way of water. Often houseplants are sold or displayed in decorative containers with no drainage, which can be especially dangerous. On the whole houseplants will need more water when they are actively growing and less when resting (possibly just every fortnight) but should be allowed to almost dry out each time. Check by inserting a finger to see if the compost beneath the surface is still moist before making any assumptions.

For almost all plants, other than succulents and cacti, a little extra humidity will always be welcome to mitigate against the dry atmosphere inside heated buildings. Misting with tepid water can help, as can placing pots on gravel trays kept topped up with water. You could also grow plants in a terrarium or bottle garden. Closed containers like this rarely need water so it is possible to grow species that like a moister, more humid atmosphere without having to mist them constantly.

Terrariums create a specialised environment for indoor plants.

CONSERVATORY
CONTAINERS

Conservatories are a compromise between the comfort of the inside and the fresh abundance of life outside, and many people like to use them as a sort of protected garden room with plants as the main feature, along with some comfortable chairs. They are ideal places to indulge a love of more unusual plants, as with care and some extra expense the conditions can be manipulated to provide the appropriate environment. Depending on the siting of the conservatory, light levels can be good, possibly too good for many plants, so shading is a consideration unless you are only interested in growing light-loving plants. Conservatories that receive sun in the morning or late afternoon only are best for all-round growing, but even those in shade can be 'greened up' with foliage plants and ferns for a lush, exotic look.

Ventilation is also a requirement. A good flow of air though the room and ventilation windows in the roof to remove excess rising heat will ensure that plants do not overheat and help prevent pests and diseases, as well as making it more tolerable for humans to spend time in. Against this, though, has to be set the need for humidity. Inside spaces can be dry, but most plants prefer a little moisture in the air. Trays of gravel and water hidden away or regular misting may be required to compensate.

This is especially important in conservatories that are heated. Naturally warmer anyway, due to their proximity to the house they may also be connected to the domestic heating system, which can be a little tricky as plants do not necessarily appreciate the temperatures that humans do. Tropical and tender plants do best in temperatures that do not drop below 13°C (55°F), so extra heat at night may be necessary. Unheated conservatories will still be significantly warmer than outside but may be a little too cool in winter for very tropical plants, in which case, concentrate on sub-tropicals and half-hardy plants, which will still give you an exotic feel but should cope with winter temperatures under 10°C (50°F), as long as they are not subjected to frost at any point. In extreme cold weather consider an additional source of heating, such as an oil-filled radiator.

Good ventilation is essential to prevent problems.

Since it is rare to come across a conservatory with integrated beds of soil, the majority of conservatory plants will have to be grown in containers, although these may be almost permanent features, such as watertight brick-built planters in larger conservatories. More usually, though, smaller, movable pots and containers are used, with saucers or trays underneath to prevent excess water runoff. This has the great advantage of flexibility. You can redesign your displays whenever you want, especially if you own a trolley to move larger plants or at least move any plants that are not happy in their position. Some plants may need to be moved occasionally anyway, as they may have periods of dormancy or rest or need a change of environment to trigger flowering.

Rather than having large, substantial plants that are heavy to move around, especially difficult if health and mobility are an issue, you could achieve a mature, well-filled look by growing smaller plants on staging or shelves of different heights.

Plant choices

In warm, well-lit environments there is a huge range of tropical beauties that can be successfully grown inside. Alien-looking *Anthurium* and rose grape (*Medinilla magnifica*) are always a talking point alongside the luscious blooms of hibiscus (*Hibiscus rosa-sinensis*), *Justicia* and *Hippeastrum*. Mix strongly shaped foliage plants such as palms and philodendron with the decorative foliage of fan plant (*Begonia rex*) and herringbone plant (*Maranta*) to suggest lush jungle. For height and scent, jasmine and stephanotis will thrive, as will bougainvillea, as long as it receives plenty of light. In slightly cooler environments brugmansias do extremely well, alongside bird of paradise, African primroses and clivias.

Where light is lower you can turn to jungle foliage plants, which, although they tend not to have the best flowers, almost inevitably have fascinating foliage. Umbrella plants and swiss cheese plants are the sort of plants that do well in poorer light.

For those with limited time or a forgetful nature, cacti and succulents are the most tolerant of all the plant families, coping with neglect better than most, although they will look much better and healthier if you do take care of them.

Orchids and bromeliads

Orchids and bromeliads are some of the most commonly available houseplants as they fit in so well with modern interior decoration yet are easy to care for, unless you have come across a particular rarity. The orchids and bromeliads usually available are what are known as epiphytes; that is they do not grow in soil naturally but attach themselves to tree branches in the wild, piggybacking on the faster-growing tree to get closer to the sun. This means there are special conditions to consider when growing them in pots. Unlike most plants they are not appreciative of being potted into moist compost and can easily rot from below. Bromeliads have mostly anchor roots and actually take in moisture and nutrients either directly from the atmosphere through their cell walls or by collecting rainwater and debris in the funnel created by the leaves. It is this 'talent' plus their extraordinary flowers that have made them deservedly popular. Rather than grow them in compost-filled pots, it is more appropriate to use a mix of bark chippings, sand and peat substitute to ensure very good drainage, or even attach them to an old branch or piece of trunk by wrapping the roots in moss and wiring the plant onto the wood for a more intriguing display. Either method will mean that you should mist your plants daily and only water them when the potting mix or moss is dry, filling up any non-flowering funnels at the same time. Tillandsias especially (often called 'airplants') sometimes have no roots at all. Spanish moss (*Tillandsia usneoides*), for example, simply hangs from trees, a tangled skein of grey draped over branches like abandoned clothing. As all bromeliads come from warm, tropical regions they prefer temperatures above 10°C (50°F) and indirect rather than direct light.

Orchids are somewhat similar. The vast majority sold are moth orchids (*Phalaenopsis*), which tolerate considerable neglect but flower for a surprisingly long time. They too have specialised roots that not only collect moisture from the atmosphere but photosynthesise, hence they are usually sold in white, transparent

Moth orchids are popular houseplants that are easy to look after.

pots in compost with a high proportion of bark chippings. Moth orchids and other epiphytic orchids, like *Dendrobium* and *Stanhopea*, also benefit from regular misting and can be grown just like bromeliads on moss-covered bark or even hanging baskets filled with orchid compost and lined with moss. Other orchids, and there are literally thousands of species and hybrids available and they grow in almost every environment, may need more specialist attention and care. Take advice from the grower if you want to buy and care for the rarer varieties.

Modern trends in indoor gardening

As society is becoming increasingly urbanised and more and more of us no longer have guaranteed access to outside spaces to grow or enjoy plants, technology and design have begun to develop new and different ideas for the twenty-first century. While scientific research is showing that there are huge health and wellbeing benefits to living close to nature, our daily lives are moving ever further away from our rural roots on the land. Yet living around plants, it appears, is soothing and relaxing for both mind and body, and even helps to keep the air we breathe clean and fresh.

Good modern design now takes account of this and there are plenty of newly built houses that integrate nature into the very fabric of the building. The great American architect Frank Lloyd Wright was instrumental in beginning this trend, and along with more recent Scandinavian design influences, this concept is having an increasing impact on workspace and interior design. Pots and containers now come in many more forms than in the past. Upside-down planters can be found that hang from the ceiling, saving space while looking distinctly space-age. Stylish self-watering pots and containers allow us to go off and enjoy life. At the top of the technological tree are the relatively new artificial growing systems using artificial light, hydroponics and even electronic sensors to grow plants on the table tops of kitchens and city apartments round the world. Who knows what may come next?

INDEX